NATIONAL GEOGRAPHIC LEARNING | CENGAGE

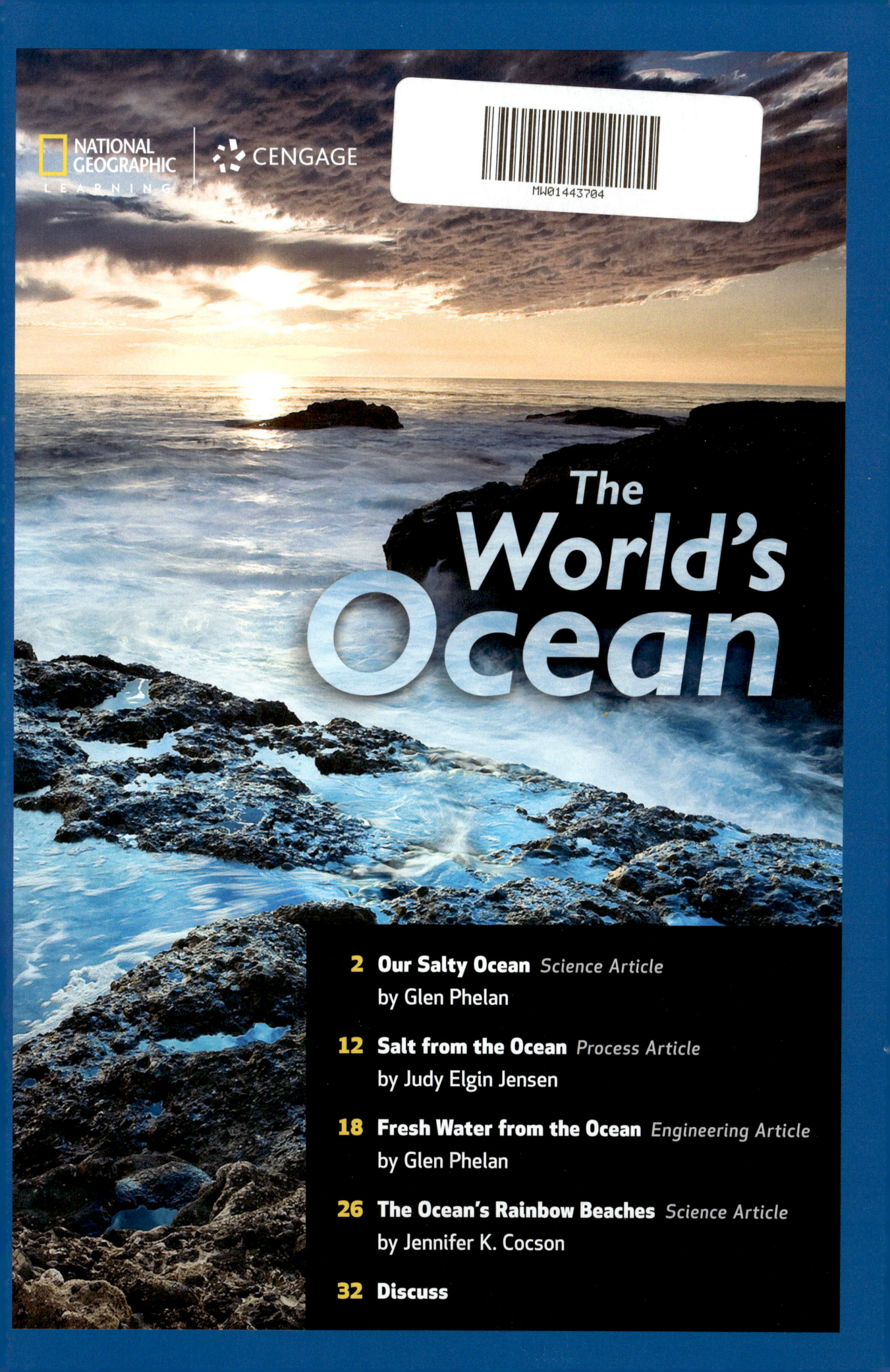

The World's Ocean

2 **Our Salty Ocean** Science Article
by Glen Phelan

12 **Salt from the Ocean** Process Article
by Judy Elgin Jensen

18 **Fresh Water from the Ocean** Engineering Article
by Glen Phelan

26 **The Ocean's Rainbow Beaches** Science Article
by Jennifer K. Cocson

32 Discuss

GENRE Science Article   **Read to find out** about properties of the vast world ocean.

Our Salt

Imagine standing on a beach and looking out to sea where water stretches before you to the distant horizon. It is your first glimpse of the ocean, and it is more water than you have ever seen. Yet what you can see is only a tiny fraction of Earth's vast ocean. The continents separate the ocean into different sections that we call the Arctic, Atlantic, Pacific, and Indian Oceans. However, they are all connected into one global ocean. The ocean is an amazing place full of life, full of mystery, and full of surprises.

Earth's "tallest mountain" honor goes to . . . Hawai'i's Mauna Kea. Although it is mostly underwater, it is actually taller than Mount Everest.

10,200m (33,465 ft.)

8,848m (29,028 ft.)

Most of the ocean is so deep that the sun's light cannot reach its depths. Angler fish that live in this darkness have glowing lures that attract prey.

2

Ocean

by Glen Phelan

Ocean water supports the huge mass of the blue whale. Earth's largest animal ever, it stretches to a length of about 2.5 school buses.

A milk jug's volume of ocean water contains 9 large spoonfuls of salt.

3

Salt Water

A mouthful of seawater can taste as salty as a mouthful of potato chips. That might not surprise you if you have ever gone swimming in the ocean. All it takes is a little splash of water on your lips—you can really taste the salt! You can feel it, too, if you splash it on a scrape or cut on your skin, ocean water can make the cut sting.

The sting comes from the salt of course. Unlike fresh water, ocean water is mostly a **mixture** of water and different kinds of salts—not just the sodium chloride that makes up table salt—but other salts as well. The salts **dissolve** or break up into particles that spread evenly throughout the water, which makes salt water a kind of mixture called a **solution**. If the salts could be removed from ocean water and spread evenly over the continents, they would form a layer 150 meters (500 feet) thick—about the height of a 40-story building.

You might be wondering how the salts entered the ocean, and, perhaps unexpectedly, most of the salts come from the land. All natural water has a little salt in it because rain dissolves salts from rocks and soil and washes them into streams that then flow into rivers that eventually empty into the ocean. Salts also enter the ocean from below—volcanoes and small vents on the ocean floor belch minerals, including salts, into the ocean water.

The entire global ocean is salty, but some parts are saltier than others. Think about the cold polar regions where some ocean water at the surface freezes into ice, forming chunks or even shelves that can be as large as a small country. When water freezes at Arctic and Antarctic temperatures, the ice is fresh water only because the salt stays behind in the liquid water, making the surrounding water saltier. Now switch to the hot tropics where a lot of ocean water **evaporates** into the warm air. As the water evaporates, becoming a gas, the salt stays behind in the liquid water, so this part of the ocean is saltier than the rest of the ocean.

Now think about what happens at the mouth of a river where it empties into the ocean. Even with carrying a little salt, the shear volume of the river's fresh water dilutes the saltier ocean water near the mouth of the river. So where the river enters the ocean, that small part of the ocean is slightly less salty than other parts.

Ice floats in water, but not right on top! Like an ice cube, most of an iceberg floats below the surface.

water line →

Close to 50,000 icebergs can be seen each year in the Arctic Ocean.

A river in Norway dumps its silt, water, and dissolved salts into a sea that is part of the Arctic Ocean. The silt, or eroded land, forms the fan shape called a delta. The water and dissolved salts mix into the ocean.

Waves

"WATCH OUT!"

It looks like a wipeout for sure as the giant wave curls over and crashes down upon the surfer. The spectators on the beach hold their breath, hoping the surfer is all right. Seconds pass with no sign. Then... there he is! The surfer emerges from the barrel—the tunnel of water that forms as the top of the wave curls over. Cheers erupt as the skilled surfer rides the wave all the way to shore.

Surfers know all about waves. They know that most waves are caused by wind, or moving air. The blowing winds drag across the surface and pass energy to the water.

In 2012, a surfer rode a record-breaking 24-meter (78-foot) wave off the coast of Nazaré, Portugal.

You might say the wind energizes the ocean as the energy passes through the water as waves.

As you can guess, the stronger the winds are, the bigger the waves are. Imagine a storm brewing out at sea with fierce winds that kick up some serious waves. The energy might take many hours to reach the coast, but when it does, the waves become walls of water taller than houses. That's paradise for the serious surfer.

Now imagine that you're out on a surfboard sitting on the board, watching the sea. Wave after wave rolls beneath you causing you to bob up and down as each wave passes. The water around you bobs up and down too. The waves move forward, but the water and things on the water—such as you—don't really move much.

Okay—enough sightseeing. Time to catch a wave. You quickly paddle forward and then stand up as the water swells beneath your board. It's a nice-sized wave, about half your height, but that's about to change.

Out of the corner of your eye, you can see that the wave has grown as tall as you and now the wall of water towers over you. What's going on? The wave is approaching shallower water. The water is shallow enough that the bottom of the wave rubs against the ocean floor, which slows the wave but also pushes it higher.

You can feel the wave's power along with some water on your shoulders. The wave is breaking! The bottom of the wave slows down more than the top does, so the top leans forward, curls, and topples over. That's about the only time that a wave actually pushes water forward. It pushes you forward too, with a sudden jolt, but you keep your balance through it all. What a fantastic ride!

Sea stars, barnacles, and other tide pool organisms can live both in and out of water.

Nearly 4,000 kinds of fish dart and glide among the reefs of the ocean.

Animals in the open ocean swim for miles in search of food.

Ocean Life

What lies beneath the ocean waves? Only the greatest variety of life on Earth! From shallow shores to the deepest waters, Earth's ocean is home to organisms of every color, shape, and size. Some organisms swim through the water, including whales, dolphins, octopuses, and all kinds of fish. Bottom dwellers, such as lobsters, corals, and sea stars, live and walk, or crawl, on the ocean floor. Jellies and many kinds of microscopic organisms are floaters, staying at or near the surface. Seaweeds might do both—float or be anchored to the bottom.

Swimmers, bottom dwellers, and floaters all are adapted to life in the ocean's salty water. For example, to avoid the unhealthy buildup of salt in their bodies, fish pass extra salt through their skin and gills.

The ocean includes many kinds of environments and each has its unique mix of life. You can explore some of these places without even getting your feet wet. Tide pools are rocky depressions along shore that are underwater during high tide and remain filled with water during low tide. The saltiness of water in tide pools increases as the water evaporates and decreases when the tide comes in or when it rains.

The greatest variety of ocean life is found on or near coral reefs. Ant-sized animals called corals produce limestone coverings that build the stony reefs in tropical waters near shores.

Some reef visitors, such as sharks, dolphins, and other larger marine animals, are more at home in the open ocean. Compare the organisms that live in the different environments shown here. This is just a tiny fraction of the huge variety of life that inhabits the world's salty ocean.

A mouthful of seawater can contain hundreds of thousands of tiny animals and plantlike organisms. Millions of bacteria live there, too. Spit it out!

In the Deep

The year was 1977. A scientist and a pilot slowly descended to the floor of the Pacific Ocean in a small research submarine called *Alvin* while another scientist kept track of *Alvin's* progress from the mother ship on the surface. They were part of an exciting expedition. The scientists wanted to find out if some of the ocean's salt was coming from volcanic vents on the seafloor. No one had ever explored these vents. This was their chance and it turned out to be the chance—and the discovery—of a lifetime.

As *Alvin* approached the ocean floor, the pilot called out, "There's clams out here!" In the submarine's spotlights, they could see a colony of giant clams, each bigger than a football, but that's not all. There were anemones, crabs, mussels, and fish. Strangest of all were the colossal worms with red tips that extended from slender white tubes. The worms were taller than a doorway and swayed like prairie grass in a breeze.

Later, when specimens were brought to the surface, one of the scientists described the worms to her colleagues over the phone. "I asked, 'Hey, can you biologists tell us what these things are?' And they said, 'What? We don't know what that is. Hold everything!'"

The scientists had discovered a world of creatures in the most unlikely place. How could all this life be flourishing here, nearly 3 kilometers (2 miles) beneath the waves—in total darkness? Without sunlight, how did the organisms get energy?

The answer lay in the nearby vents. These rocky chimneys, called black smokers, spew out a mixture of salts, minerals, chemical gases, and extremely hot water. One of these gases is food for bacteria that live inside the tube worms and other animals. The bacteria use the gas to produce chemicals that provide nourishment for the animals.

Since 1977, scientists have discovered many vents and the life that surrounds them. And in case you're wondering, *Alvin* is still going strong. It has been joined by dozens of subs and other high-tech tools for exploring the ocean. Maybe one day, you'll take a deep-sea voyage and join in the thrill of discovery.

The black plumes, rich in chemicals such as sulfur, iron, zinc, and copper, measure over 350°C (662°F)!

The bright light shining on these strange animals comes from the submarine.

Check In Why are some parts of the ocean saltier than others?

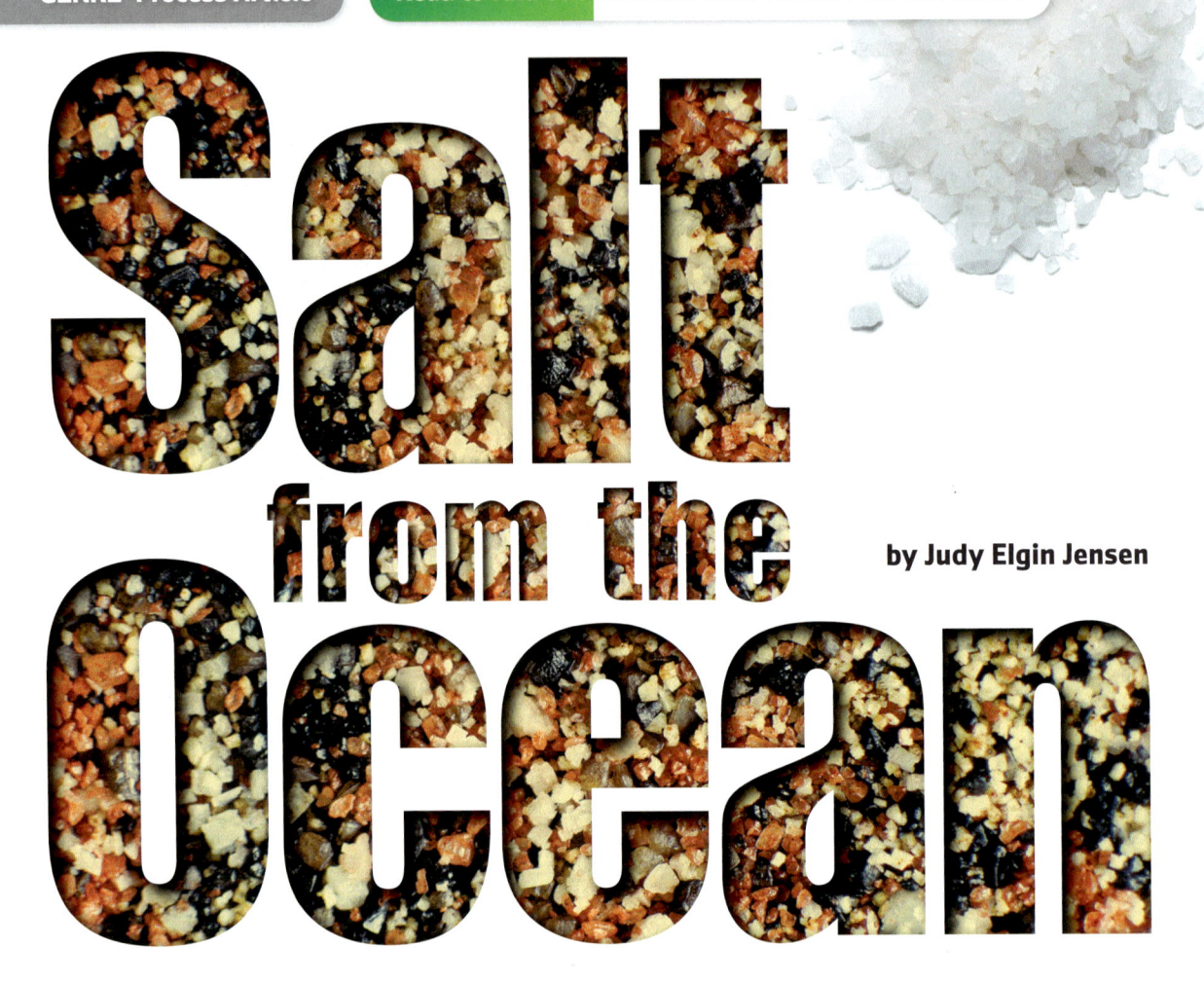

GENRE Process Article | **Read to find out** how salt is harvested from the ocean.

Salt from the Ocean

by Judy Elgin Jensen

When you reach for a saltshaker in a restaurant nowadays, you might find your fingers wrapped around a container labeled "sea salt." You'll see this kind of salt in grocery stores, too. What's so special about sea salt? And just what is it anyway?

Sea salt is exactly that—salt that comes from the sea, or ocean. The salt is harvested after seawater **evaporates** from shallow pools, leaving the salt behind. Table salt—the salt in most saltshakers—comes from underground mines.

Table salt and sea salt are not that different. They both are made of the same kinds of particles—sodium and chlorine—that combine to form sodium chloride. Many sea salts are left in large grains because coarse salt doesn't stick together, or cake, as much as fine-grained salt does. When you're ready to cook or flavor foods, you use a grinder to break the sea salt into smaller grains. Sea salt also includes tiny amounts of minerals that give the salt different flavors and colors. Chefs use these differences to enhance various foods and so do cooks at home. Here are just a few of the many kinds of sea salts available today.

Fleur de Sel That's French for "Flower of Salt," which means it's the best of the salt harvested in certain regions of France. Flavors vary slightly depending on the region.

Black Lava Sea Salt This salt is produced on the Hawaiian island of Moloka'i. It is rich in minerals and has a striking color with a slightly nutty flavor. It is blended and colored with charcoal.

Chipotle Sea Salt Made with smoke-dried chipotle peppers and Pacific sea salt, this salt has a toasted pepper flavor that makes foods taste hot and spicy.

Red Alaea Sea Salt Pacific sea salt is combined with red alaea clay from Hawai'i to color this salt crimson. This salt is rich in minerals and is used to flavor and preserve food.

French Grey Sea Salt This coarse salt is harvested from the Atlantic waters off the coast of France. It actually smells like the ocean and is naturally rich in minerals.

Apple Smoked Salt Smoked over a fire burning wood from apple trees, this flaky salt absorbs the mild fruit flavor of the wood. It also contains minerals from the sea water.

Harvesting Sea Salt

Life in the ocean needs salt water to survive and people need some amount of salt, too. You know that a lot of the salt we use comes from the evaporation of salty seawater, although it's not quite that simple.

You can't produce sea salt just anywhere, at least not on a large scale. People harvest sea salt in places where the climate is fairly warm and sunny and breezes are strong and steady. And of course, seawater must be nearby and plentiful.

Harvesting sea salt requires some people skills, too. The photos of the salt ponds here and on the next page summarize the process of harvesting sea salt on the island of Gozo, Malta, in the Mediterranean Sea. Let's see how it's done.

Step 1

First, seawater is pumped into shallow ponds, which are often made of local clay. Wind and sunlight slowly evaporate the water in the ponds. As more and more water evaporates, the remaining **solution,** called **brine**, gets saltier and saltier.

Step 2

The brine then moves through a series of ponds. After almost two years, the brine is about 25 percent salt. (Seawater is about 3.5 percent salt.) The brine is now so salty that solid crystals of salt start forming out of the solution.

Step 3

Evaporation continues over time and more salt crystals form. When the salt layer is about 10 centimeters (4 inches) thick, the salt is broken up, scooped, poured into dump trucks, and hauled off to be washed.

Step 4

At the wash plant, the salt is churned in tubs to remove sand and dirt. The clean salt may be stored in mounds. A conveyor belt carries the stored salt to another place to be crushed, dried, and packaged. Then it's off to the store and to your kitchen!

Importance of Salt

Salt is much more than a seasoning to put a little zip in your food. Entire civilizations have been impacted by these little crystals. Hundreds of years ago, Venice, Italy, became an economic power by selling salt. In the late 1500s, the Dutch prevented war from an aggressive Spanish king by blocking the transportation of salt from one of Spain's most important harvesting plants. Unable to sell this critical product, Spain went bankrupt and could not fight a war. In the late 1700s, a tax on salt in France was one cause of the French Revolution.

▽ A scale for measuring sea salt is a common tool at open-air markets. This market is in East Timor on an island north of Australia.

Sacks of local sea salts are on sale at a market on the Spanish island of Mallorca in the Mediterranean Sea.

That's not all—over the years, salt has been used as money. Soldiers of ancient Rome were paid partly in salt. In fact, the word *salary* comes from the Latin word for "salt" as does the word *salad*, which started with Romans adding salt to their leafy greens and veggies.

Why is salt so valuable? How has it had the power to build economies and influence wars? Salt is one of those substances your body needs, though in small amounts. It helps your muscles work, your blood flow, and your heart beat. Salt is also terrific for preserving food because it slows the growth of bacteria that spoil food. Salting fish and meats was especially important before refrigeration existed. This method of salting continues in many cultures today.

The popularity of sea salt has made this substance once again important to many local economies. A small, family-owned salt works in Maine extracts salt from seawater by evaporating the water in solar greenhouses. A huge commercial sea salt works outside San Francisco looks similar to those you can visit in Guatemala and around the world. From open-air markets to gourmet cooking shops and Internet storefronts, merchants compete for customers as the sea salt trend grows.

A crust of salt kept these fish from spoiling. They will be grilled and sold at a market in Bangkok, Thailand.

Check In Why is seawater pumped into shallow ponds rather than deep ponds?

17

GENRE Engineering Article **Read to find out** about a solution to a freshwater supply problem.

Fresh Water from the Ocean

by Glen Phelan

EARLY DUBAI, 60 YEARS AGO

The dust is everywhere. It gets in your clothing, your hair, your eyes. Add in the blazing sun and scorching temperatures and you have the recipe for a miserable day, but there's no sense in complaining.

That's just the way it is here in the Middle Eastern city of Dubai on the shores of the Persian Gulf. After all, this *is* a desert.

You pass a man sitting on a bench in the shade of a two-story clay building. He's watching children kick a ball in a sandy alley when the ball skirts past one of the players and comes your way. Then you see that it's not a ball at all—just a bunch of rags tied together. Who has money for sports equipment? This is a poor town where most people cannot read or write, and jobs are few. Many people barely make a living fishing for sardines in the Persian Gulf. Tents serve as houses. But the children aren't thinking of their poverty. They laugh and play as you tap the ball back to them.

You turn the corner and come nose to nose with a camel whose owner, a merchant, uses the animal to carry goods to one of Dubai's open-air markets. Colorful cloth draped over poles provides shade for people who stroll among the booths. The sweet aromas of cinnamon and cloves fill the air as do the sounds of people bickering over prices. You buy a handful of dried fruit and continue on your way.

A few minutes later you come to the small creek that snakes its way through town. Is this where people get drinking water in this dry place? No. Unlike most creeks, this one is salt water. The creek empties into the Persian Gulf, which is salt water too. Little rain falls, and no rivers and no big lakes exist that could supply fresh water. The few deep wells in town provide enough water for the 30,000 people who live here, but it's still a scarce resource.

A saltwater creek divides the city. Everywhere else is dry, desert sand.

19

DUBAI, TODAY

Pop music blares over the sound system while hundreds of storefronts invite customers to enter. You are in the largest mall in the world, right here in Dubai. People wearing traditional Arabic clothing stroll alongside teens wearing shorts and blue jeans. In addition to its 1,200 stores, the Dubai Mall has an ice rink, an aquarium, a theme park, and movie theaters—and that's just for starters. Outside are fountains and pools. Skyscrapers, including the world's tallest, line wide streets. Tourists and business people from all over the world stay in luxurious hotels. How did the dusty town become such a sparkling city?

In the mid-1960s, oil was discovered beneath Dubai's desert sands. It wasn't as much oil as in other parts of the Middle East, but it was enough to jump-start Dubai's economy. Dubai's new wealth led to new businesses, industries, and schools. People from nearby countries came to build the modern city and tourists followed. The population grew to more than a million people.

As Dubai grew, it faced a major problem—a shortage of fresh water. People needed fresh water not only for drinking but also for washing, farming, and running factories and

Peering up at the gleaming towers of glass and steel, or strolling through an indoor mall, it's hard to imagine the Dubai of 60 years ago.

power plants. Scientists and engineers came up with an ingenious way to solve the problem. They figured out how to get fresh water from salt water in a process called **desalination**.

The word *desalination* might look big, but you can figure out its meaning. The prefix *de-* means "to reverse or remove." The root word *saline* is Latin for "salt." The suffix *-ation* means "result of an action." So desalination is the action of removing salt.

Several methods exist to desalinate salt water. The Jebel Ali desalination plant in Dubai uses one based on the processes of evaporation and condensation that many large desalination plants use. You know that when water **evaporates,** salt and other minerals stay behind, so the water that evaporates into water vapor, or gaseous water, is fresh. The Jebel Ali desalination plant works by catching fresh water vapor and **condensing** it, or turning it back into liquid. The condensed water then collects in trays and is piped to storage tanks. Salty seawater from the Persian Gulf goes in and refreshing, drinkable, fresh water comes out.

Farmers in the Liwa Oasis irrigate with groundwater. The oasis is a four-hour drive from Dubai.

USING DESALINATED WATER

In parts of the Middle East, including Dubai, chances are good that the water running out of the faucet came from the sea. Most of the drinking water for these countries comes from desalination plants.

Desalinated water satisfies most other everyday needs, too. Industries use desalinated water to cool machinery and make products. Farmers sometimes use desalinated water to irrigate fields, however, most irrigation in the Middle East uses **groundwater**—water that collects between rocks and in the cracks of rocks underground. Without desalination, cities along the coast would have to pipe groundwater over long distances. If people in the cities used more groundwater, less would be available for crops.

Desalination technology, however, isn't perfect. For one thing, it requires lots of energy. Most desalination plants burn fossil fuels to heat the seawater. To reduce the pollution from burning fossil fuels, engineers have designed desalination plants that use solar energy to heat the water.

Desalination also produces a lot of **brine** that can be unhealthy to nearby ocean life. One way to solve this problem is to spread the brine out and release it more slowly, so engineers designed a system in which the brine releases gradually and mixes more safely with the surrounding ocean water.

The water released back into the ocean can be warmer than the surrounding area, too. Warmer water is less dense and holds less oxygen. Less dense water forms a layer above more dense water that can trap tiny ocean life below. Less oxygen in the water might not be enough for the natural ocean organisms. Cooling the water or adding oxygen to it before pumping it back to the sea can help. Scientists and engineers continue to study problems with desalination and design systems to provide solutions.

DESALINATION AROUND THE WORLD

Desalination is becoming more and more important in dry regions of the world. In Saudi Arabia, 30 desalination plants supply 70 percent of the drinking water. Other countries in the Middle East, such as Israel, also rely heavily on this technology for their drinkable water. Desalination plants are operating not only in the Middle East but around the world. In fact, more than 15,000 plants produce 65 billion liters (17 billion gallons) of fresh water every day! That sounds like a lot, and it is. Yet that's only about two percent of all the fresh water

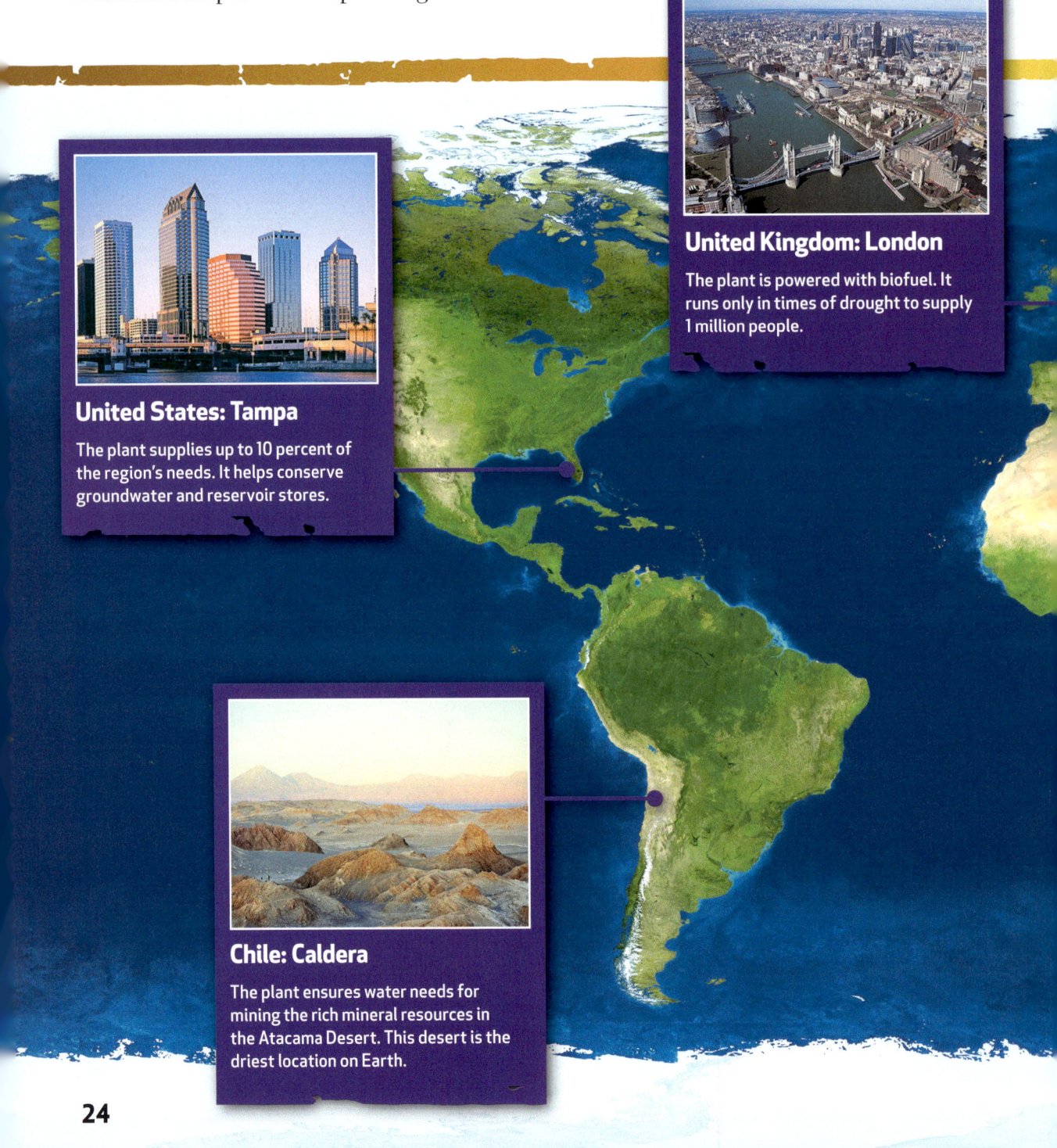

United Kingdom: London
The plant is powered with biofuel. It runs only in times of drought to supply 1 million people.

United States: Tampa
The plant supplies up to 10 percent of the region's needs. It helps conserve groundwater and reservoir stores.

Chile: Caldera
The plant ensures water needs for mining the rich mineral resources in the Atacama Desert. This desert is the driest location on Earth.

people around the world use each and every day. Although desalination plants carry a high price tag, more of them are being built. Some serve simply as backup systems to more conventional freshwater supplies, being used only in time of drought. Others sit far inland and extract salt from briny groundwater supplies or reservoirs. Improved technology is bringing down the costs as well as making desalination more environmentally friendly. Maybe someday you'll be a scientist or engineer working on the latest technology to help provide fresh water to a thirsty world.

India: Chennai
The plant supplies 4.5 million people. Water shortages result when erratic monsoons don't fill lakes and reservoirs.

Australia: Melbourne
The plant serves a growing population. Changing rainfall patterns mean reservoir stores can't keep up.

South Africa: Mossel Bay
The plant can supply all of the town's needs in case of a severe drought. Droughts are somewhat common here.

Check In What problems in the desalination process are engineers trying to solve?

GENRE Science Article **Read to find out** why beaches are different colors.

THE OCEAN'S Rainbow Beaches

by Jennifer K. Cocson

Punalu'u Beach

By now you know that seawater is much more than just water—it's a **mixture** of water, salts, minerals, gases, and microscopic life. When that watery mixture breaks on shore, it washes over another mixture—the beach. Yes, a beach is a mixture. Just scoop up a handful of it and see for yourself. You'll find sand, of course, but maybe a few shells and pebbles, too, that you can easily pick out.

Where do all these different beach ingredients come from? The shells wash up from the ocean while the rocks and sand usually come from the land nearby. Rivers carry **eroded** bits of rock from the land downstream and dump this sediment near the coast. Breaking waves smash pieces of sediment against each other, and the sediment breaks into smaller and smaller pieces—grains of sand. The crashing waves also erode the rocky shoreline, especially during fierce storms. The constant wave action works and reworks the sediment, forming a beach that is a mixture of the local rocky material.

If beach sand comes from nearby rocks, and if rocks are all different colors, shouldn't beaches be all different colors, too? They are! In fact, beaches come in a rainbow of colors. So if you thought all sandy beaches were white or light tan, you're in for a surprise. Let's take a look at some of the world's most colorful beaches.

Hawai'i in the United States is famous for its gorgeous beaches. Take Punalu'u Beach on the Big Island of Hawai'i, for instance. Its black grains are tiny bits of hardened lava. The lava flows down the volcano that forms the island. The hot lava flows into the ocean water and cools instantly into black rock called basalt that the waves pound into bits of black sand that wash up in coves to create black sand beaches, such as Punalu'u.

The black sand of this beach in Hawai'i comes from the black volcanic rock that makes up much of the island.

What makes the sand at Pu'u Māhana Beach in Hawai'i green?

Puʻu Māhana Beach

Let's stay on the Big Island for another hue. On the west side of the island you'll find a gem of a beach. Really! The sand grains of Puʻu Māhana Beach are like tiny green jewels. The olive-green color comes from the mineral olivine. Where does the olivine come from? Look up!

The cliffs that surround the beach are the remains of an old cinder cone, a hill formed by volcanic debris, and they are loaded with olivine. Rain washes bits of olivine down the cliffs while waves erode the base and wash olivine onshore. The backwash of the waves tends to sweep lighter particles out to sea and leave the heavier olivine grains behind.

The grains of olivine are too small to be valuable, but larger crystals of this mineral are the semi-precious gem called peridot.

Now hop over to another tropical island paradise—the Bahamas. Guess what color the sand is at Pink Sands Beach. Okay, that was too easy, but can you guess where the pink color comes from? It comes from the bright pink or red shells of microscopic animals that live among the nearby coral reefs. After the animals die, the waves smash the shells and wash the bits onto the shore. The ground-up shells mix in with the white sand to give the beach a pink color, especially in the wet sand at the water's edge.

Pink Sands Beach

The color of Pink Sands Beach in the Bahamas has a surprising source.

29

Rainbow Beach

Let's end our brief tour of rainbow beaches with, what else, Rainbow Beach! This colorful beach forms the edge of a large bay on the east coast of Australia. The name comes from the multi-colored sandy cliffs and dunes behind the beach. If you were to walk along this part of the coast, you might be able to count more than 70 shades of tan, yellow, orange, pink, red, blue, and brown.

A native legend tells of a spirit that took the form of a rainbow. After being killed in a fight, the spirit crashed into the cliffs, giving them their rainbow of color. The legend is an important tale in the native culture. Scientists know, however, that a mixture of different minerals is what gives the cliffs their colorful layers.

Erosion from wind and storm waves pulverizes the cliffs and forms piles of sand at the base. Wind and waves shift the sands and create an ever-changing colorful beach.

⌄ Look at all that color in the sandy cliffs of Rainbow Beach. How do you think these cliffs affect the appearance of the beach?

⌃ The sandy rainbows at Rainbow Beach in Queensland, Australia change often.

You can see some of Rainbow Beach's colorful sands on the beach surface. But the real show begins as you dig into the sand. Each swipe with your hand reveals a different combination of color—talk about sand art!

The next time you are at a beach, whether it's near the ocean or a lake, take a close look at the sand. Dig into it. Feel it. Observe what makes up this sandy mixture. Then try to figure out where the components of the mixture came from and why they look the way they do. Look around. Are there hills and cliffs? What are the nearby rocks like? What kind of minerals do they contain?

Look at a map. Does a river empty into the ocean or lake close by? What kind of land did the river flow through on its long journey here?

Whew! Those are a lot of questions. Yes, but searching for the answers is where the adventure begins!

Check In How can you predict the color of a beach by looking at the nearby landforms?

Discuss

1. Tell about some of the ways you think the four pieces in *The World's Ocean* are connected.

2. Think about the process of getting salt from the ocean described in "Salt from the Ocean" and the process of getting fresh water described in "Fresh Water from the Ocean." Identify the cause and effect in each one.

3. Explain how the physical properties of the surrounding rocks and soils impact salt in "Salt from the Ocean" and sand in "Rainbow Beaches."

4. Cite evidence from "Our Salty Ocean" for why salinity varies in locations around the world.

5. What questions do you still have about the world's ocean? What would be some good ways to find out more information?